The ADVENTURES of VIOLET the Naughty Pug

Short Stories of the Adventures of Violet the Pug

Written and Illustrated by
ALLAN NAPIER

AuthorHouse™ UK
1663 Liberty Drive
Bloomington, IN 47403 USA
www.authorhouse.co.uk
UK TFN: 0800 0148641 (Toll Free inside the UK)
UK Local: 02036 956322 (+44 20 3695 6322 from outside the UK)

This book is printed on acid-free paper.

ISBN: 978-1-6655-8973-4 (sc)
ISBN: 978-1-6655-8972-7 (e)

Print information available on the last page.

Published by AuthorHouse 06/26/2021

authorHOUSE®

Foreword

This book of short children's stories is about the adventures of our family pet Pug 'Violet.'

The idea was originally conceived in 2014 when the antics of Violet, who had just turned three years old inspired the first story of 'Violet, The Fox and Alfie.' and from then on, subsequent stories evolved.

Many of Violet's adventures include our four children's family pets (all dogs) and with whom Violet has had strong connections.

Violet came into our family as a twelve week old puppy and was officially named and registered as Miss 'Violet Havoc'. At that time no one could have perceived that some of her antics would one day find themselves as the basis of children's stories.

Violet was born with a mischievous and active mind and her second name 'Havoc', seemed somehow to personify the character she became and still remains to this day. Extremely inquisitive, of great intelligence and, single-mindedness.

Whatever goes on, Violet always appears in the thick of it!

AN 2021

CONTENTS

VIOLET, THE FOX & ALFIE

The day started brightly with the rays of the sun dancing on the walls where Violet was sleeping. Violet stretched and looked up at the ever increasing rays of the May sunshine that were now filling her little room.

Oh what a lovely day thought Violet what shall I do today. I think I will go into the woods this morning where there will be lots of lovely smells.

Violet jumped out of her bed and looked to see that no one was looking and then trotted down the garden path to a little opening in the fence that was just big enough for her to squeeze through.

It was no surprise to Violet's mummy to find her not there in her bed when she went into her room. Violet was known to be very mischievous. I wonder where that little rascal of a pug has gone now! I expect she has gone to the woods again I don't know what is so fascinating there! Oh well, I will get the children to find her later.

"Good morning Violet" said squirrel perched high in a tree. Violet stopped and looked up oh. "Oh, good morning squirrel said Violet. Where are you off to this morning, are you going to the field full of buttercups?" said squirrel. "Yes I like going there as there are lots of rabbits that I can chase," said Violet.

"You are so naughty," said a rather imperious squirrel. "One day someone will chase you!" Little did Violet think that day might be today! "Oh well enjoy yourself," said squirrel. "Bye Violet." "Bye squirrel," and Violet carried on her journey to the field full of buttercups.

Suddenly, startled by a noise Violet looked up and out jumped a baby fox cub in front of her. The fox cub looked at her and said "Is your name Violet?" to which Violet replied "yes! How did you know my name?" The little fox cub said, "I heard the children from the house calling Violet and I thought it must be you."

"What's your name little fox cub? Asked Violet "I don't really have a name" said the little fox cub. "Then I will give you one," said Violet. "Let's think! I know I will call you Freddie. You are a boy?" enquired Violet "Oh, Violet no, I am a girl fox cub!" "Then I will call you Millie."

"What are you doing today?" said the newly christened Millie. "Well, I was just on my way to the field with all the lovely buttercups and where there are lots of rabbits that we can chase," said Violet. "Would you like to come with me and we can play together?" "Oh, yes," said Millie, "I love chasing rabbits!"

So Violet and Millie trotted off to the big field full of fresh yellow buttercups where they jumped up and down and ran through the long grass chasing rabbits till they were so tired they fell asleep under a big oak tree which shaded them from the now increasing heat of the sun.

When they awoke the sun had started to disappear casting long shadows around them. "I think it's time for us to be going home," said Violet to Millie, "it will soon be dark and mummy will be mad at me for being out so long." "We foxes like the dark," said Millie, "but I expect you are right Violet, my mummy and daddy will come looking for me if I don't go home soon."

As the two friends made there way along the little path they were frightened by a loud growling noise, but they couldn't see where it was coming from. The noise got louder and louder until it became so loud that Violet cried out, "I think we are being followed!"

Violet and Millie started to run as fast as they could their little hearts beating faster and faster, but still the growling noise kept coming. "I am frightened" said Millie to Violet, "I am frightened too," said Violet. "I think it's a wolf," said Millie, "my mummy and daddy said to be careful of the wolves and here we are being chased by them!"

"Oh, what are we going to do," panted Violet, "If it gets any closer it might eat us for its dinner!" Just as the two little friends were getting exhausted, there in front of them stood Violet's big cousin Alfie. Alfie was a big boxer dog who Violet frequently tormented by running under his tummy and between his legs and occasionally she would run up behind him and nip his little tail. "Oh Alfie are we pleased to see you! There is a wolf chasing us and I think he wants us for his dinner!"

"I promise I won't torment you again said Violet if you will just save us!"

"Don't worry little Violet," said big Alfie in his deep voice. "I'll soon sort this menace out for you." "Now, let's see where this wolf," is said big Alfie disappearing into the undergrowth.

"Oh, I do hope Alfie will be alright," said Millie to Violet. "So do I Millie. He's a very brave dog to go after that wolf. I really must not tease and torment him anymore," said Violet.

As Violet and Millie were recovering from their ordeal Alfie appeared from the bushes covered in mud and twigs. "Well," said Alfie, "that's sorted him out he won't be bothering you anymore."

"Oh, Alfie we are so grateful to you for saving our lives we can't thank you enough." " Well," said Alfie, "Violet, I think it is about time you started behaving yourself and stop being naughty, your mummy has been worried about you all day, not knowing where you are, and your friend, here, her mummy and daddy will be worried too, so both of you run along home now before you get into any more trouble."

VIOLET & STANLEY

Stanley came waddling into the kitchen, "I wonder where that little pest of a pug is" he thought to himself. 'I really can't be doing with her today jumping all over me!"

Stanley was old, a very old grumpy English Bulldog. In fact it wouldn't be long before his birthday would see him turn ten years old.

Nobody seemed to know just how many homes Stanley had lived at, but for the last few years he was content, even if he had to put up with all those cats fussing around. They didn't really bother him that much, they didn't really interrupt his sleeping. Stanley liked to sleep, his main object in life was to sleep. "Fat chance of much sleep today," he thought having to come to Violet's house "she won't give me a minutes peace."

He didn't like walking either, the less exercise the better was Stanley's motto! "Now where is that little pest" he mused, as he eased himself down the step into the living room and somewhat ungraciously plonked himself in front of the large wood burner. Stanley liked to feel the warmth of the fire, "I don't suppose they will light it today for me- well it is the middle of summer," he mumbled.

"Ah well let's have a little nap before that explosion of a dog turns up," and with that Stanley closed his eyes and drifted off into the world of nod, shaken only by the sound of his loud snoring, he was oblivious to all around him. "Stanley! Stanley!" was he dreaming? "yes must be a dream," "Stanley," this time he opened one eye and there she was standing on the step about to leap on him, Violet had arrived.

"Don't you dare jump on me" he grumbled, as Violet was about to pounce.

"Oh, don't be so grumpy Stanley we can have such fun together."

"I don't want to have fun, at least not with you Violet, you are just too much. I just want a quiet life. Now run along, go away and leave me in peace."

Violet was not going to be deterred by Stanley's grumpiness as she turned around to look for her toy box. "I will get a toy for him to play with," she thought, digging into her untidy toy box and extracting a rather worn chewed teddy bear which she dropped in front of Stanley's nose.

"There, I've brought you a Teddy to play with Stanley," she said. "I do not want a Teddy Violet, in any case I'm far too old for a teddy" said an even grumpier Stanley.

"For goodness sake Stanley you won't be here for long why don't you just get up and come with me into the garden, at least you will be getting some fresh air," said Violet.

Stanley was having none of it and in no uncertain terms told Violet to stop nagging him and leave him alone as all he wanted was to sleep.

"Grumpy pants," retorted Violet. "If that's all you want to do, then do it," she said, "I will just have to play on my own" as she made her way towards the garden.

Violet wasn't put off by Stanley's rebuff. Instead she wandered towards the garden hoping that the little gate would be open so that she would have access to the flower beds and shrubbery where she liked to hide.

As she reached the big garage she noticed that one of the garage doors was slightly ajar "just enough room for me to get inside" she thought. Violet liked going in the garage, especially her daddy's workshop where there were all sorts of interesting things. Lots of things strewn around on the floor. Emerging from under the big workbench Violet had found a piece of wire wool. "That will get them going if they see me with this," she chuckled making her way out to the bright sunshine in the garden.

To her dismay there was nobody about, nobody to taunt the wire wool with! Violet liked to run up to her parents with her ill gotten gains knowing they would tell her to drop it, or leave it and then give chase when she made off. Today, nobody seemed to be around! "Oh well, that was a waste of time," discarding the wire wool on the grass. Thank goodness the little gate is open at least I have the garden to play in.

"Ah! Violet there you are," said her mummy,"I hope you haven't been annoying Stanley. You know he's old and crotchety and doesn't like to be disturbed, so don't go near him!"

Violet didn't take much notice of what her mummy was saying but kept on walking until she totally disappeared in the shrubbery and began her search for more excitement.

VIOLET & THE FROG

"Hurry along Violet," cried her mummy, but Violet was standing as though fixed to the ground. She stood there staring, her big marble like-eyes not moving, totally transfixed on an object in the tall grass.

"Will you come along Violet" her mummy called for a second time! Still Violet didn't move. She didn't even hear she was being called, so mesmerised was she at this greeny brown spotted object. Instead she leant forward, her head now in the long grass, when a croaky voice said "hello little dog," "are-are you going to eat me," said a very frightened frog.

"Eat you" retorted Violet, of course not! "I don't do things like that I want to be your friend"!

"Where have you come from?" said Violet? "I live in the stream" croaked the frog. "Well you are a long way from the stream," said Violet. "I know, I think I am lost" said the frog.

"Well, I'll help you to get back to the stream if you follow me," said a now exited Violet as she started to bound through long grass. "Come on frog, keep up" she cried! "Won't you get into trouble?" "Oh, I'm always in trouble," said Violet, "now come along."

In the distance and in fading voice Violet could hear her mummy calling "Violet, Violet where are you? Come here you naughty girl." Violet still didn't take any notice but carried on towards the stream with a now rather puffed up and puffing frog in tow.

As soon as they reached the stream a very breathless frog said "Oh thank you thank you for getting me back to the stream I will not forget your kindness Violet.

You had better get back to your mummy now, perhaps we could meet soon and play," said the frog. "That will be great," said Violet, "I know where you live now so as soon as I can get away I will come and find you."

With that Violet bounded off again to where she could hear her mummy calling.

"Where have you been?" said her mummy. "You are so naughty to keep running off. One day you will get yourself into trouble! You must realise Violet that not everyone wants to be your friend."

"Now let's get you home before you get into anymore trouble Violet." With that, Violet trotted beside her mummy showing how obedient she could be if she tried hard enough.

All Violet could think about was her new froggy friend and how she could get back to play with him. She had to plot her next adventure! She knew that if she could get away, without being seen, the hole in the fence at the bottom of the garden was her escape route.

Violet didn't have to wait long for the opportunity to arise. It was a very warm day, in fact the temperature was set to go even higher.

Her mummy and daddy thought they would make the most of the lovely weather by sitting in the garden with a Bottle of chilled white wine.

"Where's Violet?" she heard her daddy say, "I think she's in her bed indoors," her mummy replied, "it's too hot for her out here."

This was the moment Violet was waiting for as she quietly left the cool of the house, a quick dart to the flower bed across the garden path and down to the hole in the fence, nobody would notice if she was quiet.

A quick look round as she neared the hole, all was quiet, nobody had seen her as she crept through the hole and was gone into the thick foliage and cover of the woods.

Her trip to the stream in search of frog was uneventful. It seemed that the scorching heat had sent everyone to look for shelter away from the rays of the afternoon sun.

"Frog, Frog are you there?" called Violet, as she stood on the riverbank at the point where she had safely delivered frog back only a few days ago?

There was no reply from Frog. In fact the eerie silence made Violet shiver somewhat. She had a feeling of unease so much that she turned to run home when out of the rushes appeared what seemed to Violet a huge wet slimy creature.

This creature frightened Violet as it was bigger than Violet. "Who are you?" said Violet in a very trembling voice. "I am the water rat," came the reply as little globules of water dripped from his whiskers! His two front teeth seemed enormous to a now shaking Violet.

"Would you like to come into my home and see my children?" said the rat. "There's a hole in the stream bank just below us? said rat in a very insistant voice.

"No, No thank you," replied Violet in a voice that shook with fright and was barely audible.

"Oh, but I insist that you come," said rat reaching for Violet's collar tugging her with it.

"Leave me alone," cried Violet! "You are frightening me!"

This did nothing to deter the rat as he pulled harder and harder at Violet's collar. Violet seemed helpless against such a strong rat.

She dug her feet into the ground but the wet mud did nothing but make her slide as the rat pulled and pulled her towards his watery home in the side of the bank. Close by and unbeknown to Violet sat her friend, frog, who became so annoyed at what he was seeing pumped himself up to almost twice his size.

With an enormous leap in the air came crashing down on top of rat with such force that all rat could do to protect himself was to release his hold on Violet and fall sideways at which point frog hit him with a huge stone rendering rat unconscious. "There," said frog, "he won't try to do that again in a hurry!"

Violet was in a state of shock, she could hardly move and shook as frog tried to comfort her. All she could think about was what her mummy had said only days beforehand about getting herself into trouble if she kept being naughty!

After Violet had regained her composure she thanked frog for his bravery in saving her.

Frog in the meantime had gone back to his normal size. "Well," he said, rubbing his two front legs together these rats think they own the place and need to be shown that we must all live together in harmony."

"I only came to play with you frog," said Violet but I think I've had enough excitement for today and want to go home now." Of course said frog! I am pleased that I could repay your kindness of the other day! We will play together soon and who knows rat might play as well when he gets over his headache Violet said farewell to frog with a promise that she would return soon and quietly made her way home.

VIOLET & HARVEY

"Violet, Violet what are you doing now" cried her mummy, "You are always up to some mischief or other!"

Violet, was just over a year old and for some reason her mummy named her Violet Havoc as she had a feeling that the second part of her name would become rather more apt than Violet.

By the time her mummy arrived on the scene Violet was happily emptying the laundry bin in the bathroom. "I don't know what I'm going to do with you Violet, I can't leave you on your own for one single minute without you getting up to something."

"You have your cousin Harvey coming to play with you later, so I hope you won't lead him astray."

Harvey, a miniature schnauzer was younger than Violet with bushy whiskers and even bushier eyebrows. Violet always thought that he reminded her of someone but couldn't remember who.

Violet wandered out of the bathroom picking up a small nail brush that someone had let slip on the floor. This will do for a good chew thought Violet. This went unnoticed by her mummy. Another trophy for my collection, Violet thought.

"I will have some fun with Harvey later but I must have a good think as to where we can go and what we can get up to."

Before Violet arrived with her new family the daddy had fenced off the garden so Violet could not escape, but Violet with her ever increasing inquisitive mind found one little spot in the fence that had been missed. She had to squeeze herself through by breathing in but she had succeeded. So her visits to the woods became more and more frequent.

"Harvey will be able to get through this little hole, he's a lot thinner than me, so that's where we shall go."

It didn't take Violet long to make up her mind. "I know we will go to the woods" she decided.

The woods held a particular fascination for Violet even after once being chased by a wolf. They were like a magnet always drawing her back. The wolves were long gone now, her big cousin Alfie the boxer dog had seen to that. It was Alfie who saved her life along with Millie her fox cub friend.

Violet was rather surprised to see a small car pull into the drive, I haven't seen one like that before she mused. She was even more surprised to see her Aunty get out of the driver's seat. "Hello you little rascal" said her Aunty. "What are you up to now, come here and give me a cuddle.

Violet really loved her Aunty but her mind was more on this little car that had arrived in her drive. It wasn't long before her curiosity got the better of her and she sneaked off to look again at this little car.

"What are you looking at" said the car to Violet in a very rough tone that made Violet jump. "I haven't seen a car like this before" said Violet in a somewhat timid voice." Well you have now" said the little car rather gruffly.

"What's your name?" said the little car to Violet.

"Violet" she replied a little more confidant now. "What sort of dog are you anyway" enquired the little car. "I am pug" said Violet.

"A pug, you can't be" said the little car "I'm the pug" he blurted out, "there can't be two pugs." Well, as we are both pugs can't we be friends" enquired Violet, "and why do you speak so gruffly?" The little car looked at Violet and replied, "well there are a lot of bigger cars who look down on me and push me about. I am really Beetle but they all call me Pug." "Well I'm a lot smaller than you" said Violet "can't we be friends." "Well, I suppose we could try" said the little car in not such a gruff voice.

"You can call me Violet and I will call you Pug"

Violet noticed almost immediately that the tone in Pugs voice had changed, the gruffness had gone and she was sure that she now had a new friend.

"What are you doing today then?" said Pug to his new little friend? "Well, I'm waiting for cousin Harvey to come and play" replied Violet. "Why don't we all play together' said Pug?

"I thought Harvey and I would go into the woods there's a hole in the fence that no one knows about, but I think you are too big Pug to get through it". Pug thought about it hmm.

"I think you are right and it would not do for me to get scratched so soon after being bought. "Bye the way, Pug, how old are you?" said Violet. Pug thought this question was likely to rear its head. "Oh well I might as well tell you I'm Fourteen!" "Fourteen" said Violet, "my word you are quite old aren't you I am only one and cousin Harvey is a few months younger than me. Well it doesn't matter we can still have some fun can't we Pug" said Violet.

"Violet, where are you" called mummy! "I'd better go now Pug," said Violet "otherwise I will be in trouble." As Violet turned to go Pug called out "why don't we all play together later Violet when Harvey arrives. Yes, good idea" said Violet "see you later."

Harvey came bounding in tail wagging, "Hi Violet! Let's play?"

"Just a minute Harvey," said Violet, "I want to talk to you."

"You sound very serious Violet" said Harvey. "Well it's like this she replied in a very quiet tone, "we have a new friend and his name is Pug,"

"Pug" shouted Harvey, "you're a pug Violet!"

"Shush," whispered Violet, "we don't want everyone to hear Harvey. Yes, I know I am a pug, but this pug is a little car- didn't you see it in the drive."

"Doesn't look like a pug to me" replied Harvey.

"What's more Harvey he wants to play with us."

"Wow" exploded Harvey, " that will be great fun." "But nobody is to know or Pug will be in big trouble." Why's that Violet?" "Well he's only just arrived in the family and if he starts going off to play every five minutes they may think they've bought a car too naughty to keep."

Violet, in the meantime was keeping a very close eye on the situation indoors waiting for the right moment for her and Harvey to sneak away. It wasn't long before the moment arose and the two dogs crept round the side of the house to where Pug was waiting in the drive.

"Hello Pug' said Violet, "this is Harvey and we've come to play now." "Good" said Pug, "let's go for a drive. Hop in you two and don't forget to fasten your seat belts." "Let's go" said Pug, "before anybody spots us!"

With that Pug quietly reversed out of the drive and was soon negotiating the winding lane. "Where are we going Pug," said Violet, "What about the forestry land where there is a nice drive for me" said Pug, "but you will have to open the barrier to let me in."

"I like it there" said Violet, "you will like it too Harvey." So the little car with the two little dogs wound their way up the hill to the forestry land.

"Here we are" said Pug, "open the barrier for me will you?"

Violet and Harvey jumped out and started tugging at the rope attached to the long barrier. "Here it goes" said Harvey as the big arm lifted and Pug drove through.

"If you two would like to go off and play, I will carry on down the drive but make sure you can see me at all times," said a rather concerned Pug.

With that Violet and Harvey scuttled off into the undergrowth excited at being free to do just what they want.

"Violet," Harvey said, "Pug told us to keep sight of him at all times I think we may have gone too far into the woods." "Hmm. I think you are right Harvey I can't see Pug anywhere!"

"I think we are lost Harvey," said a now concerned Violet, "I don't know where we are!"

"Oh dear Violet I'm frightened" said a sad looking Harvey his usual upturned whiskers were somehow now drooping. "Oh, don't worry Harvey we will find Pug just you follow me."

Violet and Harvey made their way back along the path which they thought they had come along, but it soon transpired that there were lots of little paths and they were now totally lost.

"This is bad Harvey" said a now frightened Violet, "I don't know where we are and it's starting to get dark and nobody knows our whereabouts."

"Let's try another path" said Violet. "But just as they turned to another path, there in front of them stood a massive stag with big antlers!

"Hello stag" said Violet in a trembling shaking voice, "We are lost can you help us please?"

"I know you are lost" said the stag licking his lips, "I've been watching you for some time little dogs, ha ha ha I am going to take you back to my herd, I think we are going to have some fun with you two."

A now very concerned Violet pleaded "Oh, please don't hurt us we only came here to play" said a very shaking Violet!

The giant stag made towards them. Violet shouted "run Harvey," and the pair of them charged off into the undergrowth with a now irate and snorting stag in hot pursuit.

Just as their breath was giving out there came this horrendous noise of hooting and lights flashing ahead of them. A very scared Violet and Harvey skidded to a halt not knowing what was going to happen to them now!

From behind came an enormous crash and they were showered in tree bark and leaves. When they looked to see what was happening there was the giant stag his antlers cradled round a tree his eyes looking dazed, "what's happened to me" cried a very sad looking stag?

Violet soon realised that the noise came from Pug. The little car had saved them from the threat of the stag.

"Oh thank you oh thank you" said both Violet and Harvey as they moved towards Pug.

Pug was not in a good mood.

"I told you two to keep me in sight, but, no you had to run off! Well, don't well me" said Pug as Violet tried to interrupt, "I had to drive into the woods to find you and scratched my paintwork in so doing. Look at my wheels, I am in real trouble now, I was only bought a few days ago."

"Get in the car" said a now very gruff Pug, "let's get you two home before anything else besets us!"

With that and with two very quiet dogs Pug drove home.

UGH KIDS!

VIOLET & BELLA

"Violet I have some news for you," said her mummy! Violet with her customary nodding of her head from side to side was full of attention. "You will have a friend staying with you for a whole week so I want you to be on your best behaviour and don't, please don't, pester the the life out of her!" "Her," thought Violet "who is this friend?"

At that point the telephone started to ring and Violet's mummy went off to answer it, still leaving Violet in the dark as to who was this mysterious friend.

Violet's mummy replaced the telephone and went about her business not realising that she hadn't told Violet just who was coming to stay. Violets curiosity was getting the better of her and she kept pawing her mummy.

"Oh dear Violet what on earth is the matter, why do you keep pawing me?" she then suddenly realised that she hadn't told Violet who was coming to stay for a week. "Violet, I'm so sorry I've forgotten to tell you who is coming to stay with you - it's your cousin Bella!"

"Oh Bella," thought Violet she's the new Bulldog who has taken poor old Stanley's place since he died. "Violet thought about Stanley for a few moments, he didn't really like me, I know he was old and crotchety but I did rather tease him."

"As I said Violet, please give Bella time to settle in as she hasn't stayed here before and she might fret a little. I'm going to put the gate up to separate you at night and also when we go out."

"Hmm. Typical," thought Violet, "they don't trust me. Well, I probably do give them the run around at times, but I can't help being me."

To Violet's surprise Bella turned up earlier than expected. "Great," said Violet to Bella, "let's go outside and chase around."

Without further asking, Bella charged off leaving Violet almost speechless. Violet soon joined in and they ran and ran, round in circles chasing each other until they all but fell down exhausted.

"Let's rest for a while Bella," said a very puffing Violet. Both Violet and Bella were panting and snorting, mouths open and tongues out regaining their breath. "It's because we are both short nosed dogs that we cannot breath properly," said Bella in a very wheezing voice.

"Yes, I know Bella," said Violet in an even croaker voice, "it gets worse with the warmer weather and the long grass in the fields." "Come on you two" called Violet's mummy, "come and eat your dinners before you go on your last walk before bed."

"Oh, dear Bella, I didn't realise it was so late let's eat and we can think about what we are going to do tomorrow." With that Violet and Bella set about eating their dinners which they soon gulped down.

"Right," said Violet's daddy "time for your walk, come here you two while I put your leads on." With that, and with both Violet and Bella suitably attached they all made their way out of the house, through the churchyard and into the fields Violet was released from her lead and went charging off into the long grass. Bella was still safely attached and had to run on the extended lead.

"Don't know why I'm not allowed to run free," said a somewhat disgruntled Bella. "I think it's something to do with you running off," said Violet, "I overheard your mummy saying something about not letting you off the lead because you might decide to go off and do your own thing."

"That's brilliant," said Bella, "how are we going to do things together if I'm 'shackled' up all the time? Don't worry," said Violet, "I'll think of something." With the walk over they returned home only to hear Violet's mummy's voice saying, "bedtime now no more messing about there's good dogs."

"Bella your bed is under the table, Violet, yours as usual at the side of the Aga." " I'm not going to separate you two tonight, so I want you both to behave, especially you Violet!" her mummy said!

This delighted Violet as she didn't like being restricted as it affected her activities. So there was no huffing and snorting as she wandered off, to find her toys in her now very overfilled toy box.

"Bella, Bella, are you awake?" whispered Violet. "Don't make a noise otherwise they will hear us." Yes, Violet," yawned a very sleepy Bella, "what do you want in the middle of the night, can't you sleep?"

I was just thinking about tomorrow and what we should do," said Violet. "Let's sort it out in the morning please Violet I really am too tired right now to think about it."

"Very well then," said Violet as she sauntered back to her bed.

Violets mind was racing by now and sleep wasn't in her, "I've got to get Bella to the hole in the fence before anyone realises we've gone." A plan was gradually forming in Violet's head, "I know as soon my parents come down in the morning they are bound to send us out whilst they make their tea and probably go back to bed to drink it."

As soon as they open the door we will go straight to the hole in the fence and escape, they won't miss us, probably think we are playing in the garden.

The plan was firmly set in Violet's head now as she turned over and went to sleep. It didn't seem to Violet that she had been asleep long before she was aroused by a thunderous noise!

"My Goodness what's that noise she thought," somewhat startled! It soon dawned on her - Bella was snoring. "For goodness sake Bella," shouted Violet, "you will wake the whole house with that noise."

"What, What," said a sleep aroused Bella, "what's the matter?"

"The matter shouted Violet, you are snoring so loudly the plates on the walls are shaking, you will wake up the household if you keep that racket up." "Sorry," said a very sad looking Bella, "didn't mean to."

"I know you didn't," said Violet, "but your snoring was rather loud." "I think I get it from my dad," said a yawning Bella, "he snores so loudly, mummy says he could snore for England whatever that means!"

"It will be morning soon," said Violet, "as soon as they come down to let us out I want you to follow me to the bottom of the garden where there is a hole in the fence which leads us into the fields. We can have some fun there, so be ready!"

It didn't seem that long before Violet was aware of noises upstairs. "Ah they must be awake" she thought just as the door into the lounge opened. "Morning you two, sleep well?" said Violet's Daddy.

"Come on now into the garden," he said. Violet jumped up immediately but Bella had to struggle her rather rotund frame before waddling off after Violet. "Come on Bella be quick," shouted Violet.

Violet was first to arrive at the hole in the fence waiting for Bella to make an appearance. As Bella arrived the look on her face was of utter horror, "what's the matter Bella," enquired Violet?" "there is no way I'm going to get through that little hole," she said. " I can't make it any bigger Bella or they will guess what I've been up to and seal it off completely," said a somewhat despondent Violet.

"I think that's the end of our adventure for the time being Bella," said a now morose Violet. " Don't worry Violet, it's always good to be taken for a walk, would be even nicer if I could be let off the lead," Bella replied.

It was just after lunch the call came. " Come on you two," Violet's mummy shouted, "time for your walk, we will go over the fields and you Bella can have a run on your own today, provided that is you promise me that you will not disappear!" "Oh great thought Bella it will be nice to have a run." Bella's idea of a run normally meant a long roll on her back more often than not. Today was not going to be any different, or so she thought as they walked through the grassy fields that were well overdue for cutting. Violet's mummy unhooked the lead from Bella who ran into the long grass and immediately turned on her back rolling from side to side.

Then, without warning Bella started to roll over, and over, and over gaining speed as she tumbled down the bank through the nettles and splash into the ditch of running water landing on her back   firmly wedged between the banks and unable to move! "Help, Help," called Bella as she struggled to right herself but she was unable to move in any direction. "Oh, I'm stuck solid and nobody can hear me or knows where I am," cried a now tearful Bella.

"Where's Bella Violet?" said her mummy. "I don't know, she went into the long grass over there somewhere," said Violet pointing in the direction she last saw her. "go and look for her will you and I will follow you," said a now somewhat concerned and irate Violet's mummy.

"I know it was wrong to let her off the lead she thought, but she does need to let off steam sometimes." Violet charged down the bank towards the nettles and trees, and, hearing the sound of running water coming from the ditch made her way along the bank's side.

"There she is, oh, dear she's stuck!" cried Violet.
With that Violet's mummy arrived. "Oh, my goodness Bella what's happened, just look at you! Let me get my arms under you, I will have to lift and turn you." With one big heave Bella was turned and now stood in the running water which tickled the underside of her tummy.
"Well, Bella let's get you home I think you've had enough excitement for one day, I think for the whole week!" Bella, now firmly hitched to her lead trotted alongside Violet as they all went home.

VIOLET AT HOME

"Who's turn is it to make the tea today?" said Violets Mummy, "yours!" retorted her rather grumpy husband.

"It's always mine" she replied, "its about time you made it! "Oh, alright," he said, and with that slipped out of bed, putting on his dressing gown with almost robotic movements.

"Where's my slippers?" he shouted walking along the landing, "I don't know, although I did see Violet with them yesterday," replied his wife. The door to the dressing room was slightly ajar, and there under the bed was a slipper, but only one. "Ah ha," he thought "at least we are going in the right direction" as he pulled on the slipper. "I wonder where the other one is, as if didn't know," descending the stairs with a rather lopsided walk.

"Morning Violet," he said as he went into the kitchen. Violet with one big marble like eye greeted him with a shake of her tail and a very long stretch of her body.

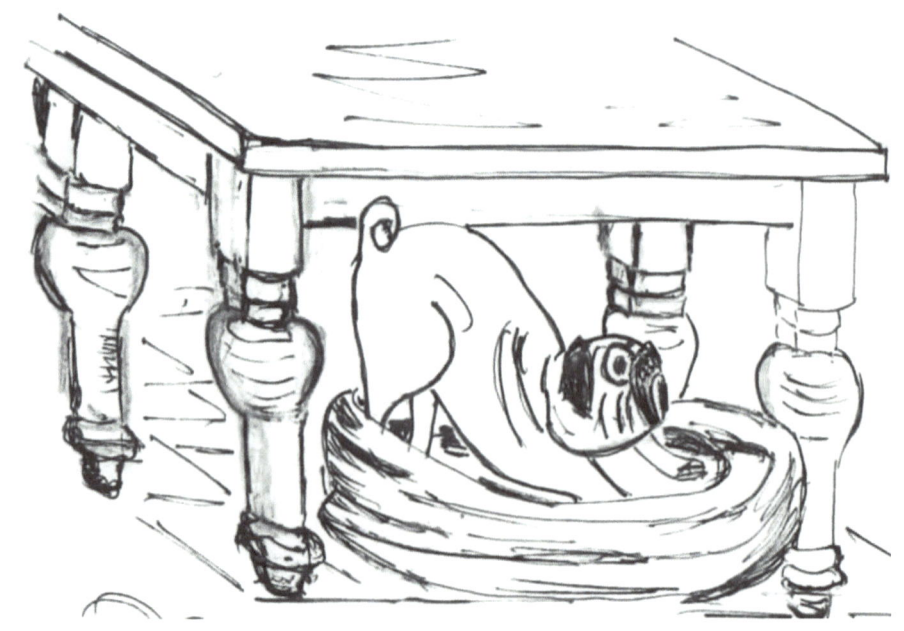

"Have you seen my other slipper?" he said walking straight to her toy box to retrieve it. "Hmm. Up to your tricks again you little rascal," he said, "come on out you go in the garden to stretch your legs."

Reticently, Violet lifted herself from her bed and with long stretching walks went slowly into the garden.

It was a nice warm morning and Violet particularly liked this time of day as the smells seemed somehow even fresher as they had recently moved house to be nearer the sea. This time she spent even longer out there until she heard her daddy's voice calling, "Violet, Violet, where are you?"

"Oh, I'd better go back in before he comes looking for me," she thought and with that trotted slowly to the back door smudging the glass with her nose.

One of Violets favourite tricks was to try and beat whoever was making the morning tea to the door and hence up the stairs to the bedroom.

This morning was no exception when her Daddy said, "I'm just taking the tea up to mummy so you stay here like a good girl." "Me a good girl," thought, Violet "watch me," and with that Violet was gone just as soon as the door was opened a few inches.

Her daddy could hear her bounding feet across the bedroom floor before he reached the stairs and his wife's voice saying, "hello you little rascal," as Violet leaped up against the side of the bed.

"Quick, quick get the waste bin before Violet gets to it!- too late," moaned her mummy, as Violets head was now retrieving and shredding tissues from it!

"Oh no," shouted Violets mummy as Violet then left the toilet with the toilet roll fixed firmly in her mouth and was now unravelling it as she made her way along the landing and down the stairs.

"Please take her downstairs and give her some breakfast will you whilst I clear up all this mess!" said Violet's mummy with a pained look, as her husband tried to grab hold of Violet. Violet slipped his grab and with a mischievous look on her face of 'come and get me' as she dropped to her front paws for a quick getaway, so the game began, as her daddy tried, and tried to catch her. Try as he might Violet had no intention of being caught and so dodged around in circles and from side to side, until her Daddy said, "Oh, I give up."

In a stern tone of voice. "Violet, that's enough of this larking about. If you don't stop now I am going to get annoyed. Now go downstairs and I will get your breakfast!"

Violet, thought, "perhaps I'm pushing my luck a bit," and scuttled off downstairs into the kitchen to await her breakfast.

Her daddy opened the fridge door and retrieved her breakfast, he'd prepared the previous evening. "Now Violet, make sure you eat it all up and please do not sort out and leave your medication as you have a habit of doing lately."

Violet was ravenous by now, and quickly tucked into the food now in front of her. " As he's reminded me of my pills she mused," I'll just see if I can find any!" She pushed the food around the dish with her very large tongue before one of her three daily pills was soon located and with one flip was deposited under the nearby box of garden shoes!

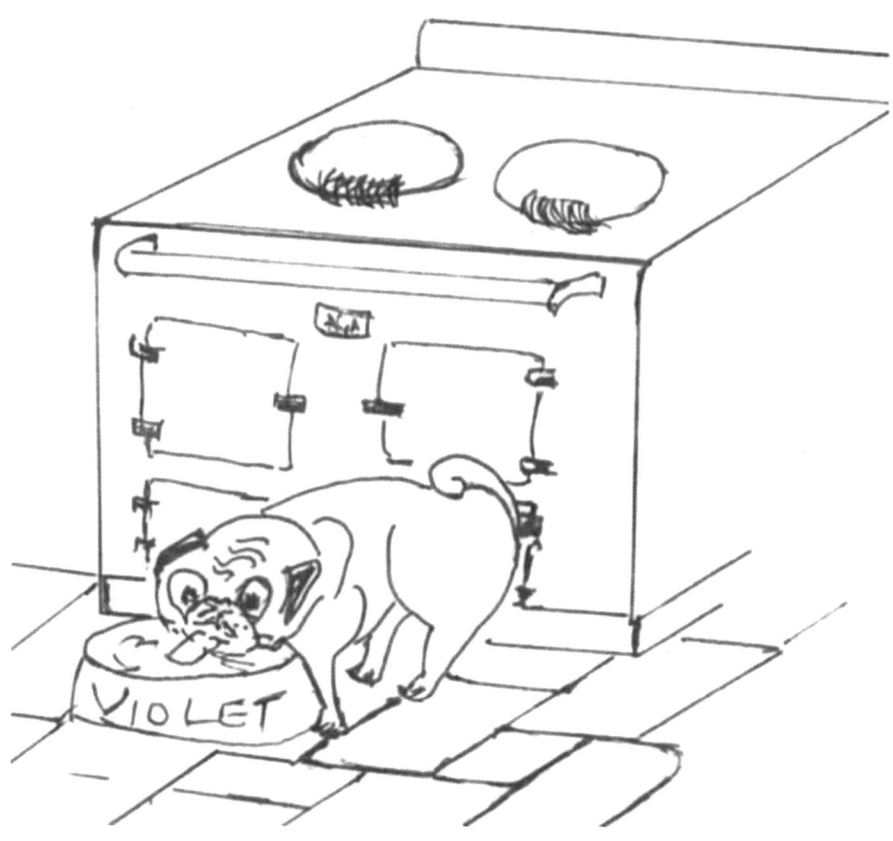

Breakfast out of the way Violet was ready now for what the day might bring. She paced up and down the kitchen, then wandered into the hall keeping a hopeful eye on the front door just in case the doorbell rang when she would make a dash in the hope of making a getaway to the outside. "What's the matter Violet you've got ants in your pants," her mummy said. " I'll take you out shortly, just be patient,"

"We'll take her down to the beach, I think the tide's out so we can go on the sands and give her a good run," her Daddy said. " great," thought Violet I love it there.

Returning home after a very 'wind blown' trip to the beach Violet was ready for her sleep after her vigorous run on the sands and made her way to one of numerous beds she had around the house. Settling into the deep fur she was soon into the land of dreams.

"Come on Puggy wake up, it's your dinner time," "Am I being called or am I dreaming," Violet thought, Again the words raced through her foggy mind "Puggy come on Pugs, I've put your dinner down for you," this time she realised the sounds of her daddy's voice."he's the only one who calls me Puggy."

With a long stretch and and even longer yawn. Violet sauntered into the kitchen for her dinner.

She finished her dinner and wandered into the lounge still wiping her face with her tongue, her mummy and daddy were sitting watching the television.

At that point a dog, no, three dogs appeared on the screen! "What are these animals doing in my house I'll soon get rid of them," as she lunged towards the big television at full speed only to hear the cacophony of sound of both her parents shouting together.

"Violet, Violet, no! no! Stop!" By which time Violet was skidding to a halt barking furiously at the animals as they gradually disappeared from view. "In your bed, in your bed," she heard her mummy saying, "stop being so naughty" her daddy cut in.

"Naughty? me?" Thought Violet.

Worn out at last!

VIOLET, BATMAN & BADGER

It was another very wet day. The rain poured from the dark heavy clouds that rolled and swirled in the skies overhead, as the winds blew in gusts that made it almost difficult to stand up. The incessant rain was coming down in torrents with such force, to see through it was a major difficulty.

"Not a day to be outside." thought Violet as she peered through the big glass windows.

"Violet," she heard her mummy call, "Violet you must go out in the garden, you can't keep putting it off! Come here and I'll put your coat on" At this point Violet knew there would be no putting it off any longer, she had to go.

"All right then," she replied, waiting for the coat to be pulled over her head. "There you are, try not to be too long," her mummy said. As her mummy opened the door it was almost snatched from her hand by the violent wind. "My goodness," she cried as Violet slid through the narrow opening.

For once Violet didn't hang about and was soon back indoors, in the dry.

"Violet I have just heard that your cousin Batman is coming today,"said her mummy. " Is Bella coming too," enquired Violet?"

"No, her Daddy has taken her fishing, and Batman won't have anyone to play with, so his mummy is bringing him here to see you. As it's raining so hard the two of you will have to play indoors," said Violet's mummy.

"Well! I don't envy Bella being out in this weather!" Thinking ahead of Batman coming. Violet was hoping that the rain might stop so that they could get outside. As was normal for Violet, excitement was brewing inside her as she paced up and down awaiting the arrival of her cousin.

Violet liked to play with Batman as he was more her size and of similar age. Batman, a French Bulldog had ears that stood up and similar facial features to both Violet and Bella his sister who was a big English Bulldog.

Violet and Batman sat side by side in front of the patio doors watching the rain unleash its venom on all who stood in its way! "I wish it would stop," said Violet, "me too, the one day I come to see you Violet and this happens." said a disconsolate Batman. However, It wasn't long before the two cousins had their wish.

Gradually the torrential rain that had threatened their enjoyment started to ease, the skies brightened and the sun's long awaited rays pushed through the clouds and the rain came to a sudden halt. " Hooray," cried out Batman! "We can go in the garden now,"said a very relieved Violet.

With no more ado Violet & Batman made their way to the back door, Violet calling out to her mummy on the way "we're going out now."

"Don't get into any mischief," she shouted back. Neither Violet or Batman heard her words as they had already gone, charging up the garden at breakneck speed before coming to a sliding halt by the back fence.

"I've got an escape route Batman," Violet pointing to the hole under the fence.

"Wow" said Batman, "do you use it very often" Batman enquired.

"Only when friends or cousins come," said Violet. "shall we go to the Fire Hills, there's plenty of room to play and with the gorse bushes no one is likely to see us," said a very excited Violet. "Won't your mummy miss us?" said Batman. "No, she thinks we are in the garden, she will call us when it's dinner time." Said Violet already preparing to slide under the fence. " Come on Batman let's go!"

As the two cousins made their way towards the Fire Hills the sun made a full appearance, it's warmth gradually drying the results of the earlier deluge.

Violet and   Batman made their way through the gorse that covered large areas of the Fire Hills to where the Spring ferns were slowly showing their new shoots.

Violet sat down to regain her breath, as Batman wandered around examining his new found playground. Batman started wandering and found himself standing on a very steep slope where he could see the waves of the English Channel raging towards the shore, whipped up by the winds. As he made his way along the slope he came across a very large opening, large enough for him to walk in.

His curiosity was getting the better of him as he crept slowly inside the hole going deeper and deeper.

It was very dark inside, his paws were now slipping on the very wet surface until he could no longer grip and slipped further into the hole skidding his way down a tunnel landing in a very wide chamber.

Batman looked around and there to his amazement and almost touching his nose was the a very large creature with white stripes. With a very cross expression on his face! "what are you doing here in my home?" said the creature.

Batman was now frightened and in a very shaky voice replied, "I am so sorry I saw the hole and my curiosity made me look deeper and then I slipped and couldn't grip and ended here."

"What's yours name?" said the creature?"

"Batman," he replied.

"Batman! that's a funny, how did you get a name like that?" said the creature. "I think it's something to do with my sticky up ears."

Batman replied. "What's your name?" Enquired Batman.

"I am Badger" he replied.

"Oh Badger I've seen lots of you around at night time,"said Batman.

"That's right we sleep during the daytime and come out to feed at night, has it stopped raining?" enquired Badger.

"Yes it's nice and sunny now," said Batman. " I came out with my cousin Violet who's a little Pug and I expect she's worried where I am."

"Let's try and get you out in the first instance Batman. I will need to go out and get help and something to pull you out with."

Violet, in the meantime was frantically searching for Batman calling "Batman, Batman where are you?"

Violet didn't hear any reply to her calls and was now worried for his safety! "What am I going to do?" thought Violet as she made her way alongside a very steep bank.

To her surprise that made Violet jump, she came came face to face with a Badger.

"Are you Violet?" Enquired Badger.

"Yes I am," said Violet.

"Your Cousin Batman is stuck in my set," said Badger.

"Set," said Violet curiously.

"Sorry, that's my home, but he can't get out as it's too slippery," said Badger.

"What are we going to do then?" Said Violet. " I was on my way to get help, and a rope or something that I can tie to his collar. As you are here now Violet you can help as well. If I attach the rope to his collar and you pull from up here I will push from behind."

"Of course Badger," said Violet.

Badger quickly returned with the rope, giving Violet one end as he disappeared into a large hole. It wasn't long before Violet could feel something happening on the end of the rope in the hole Violet took her end of the rope in her jaws and started to pull and pull and pull! It was getting heavy now and Violet tried hard to retain a grip. She almost fell over as the rope went slack and there stood Batman looking sadly at her. "Oh am I pleased to see you Batman, I've been so worried," said Violet.

"I am very sorry Violet it was all my fault but I have to thank Badger for helping to get me out!" There, standing behind Batman appeared Badger, "I am so happy everything had turned out well," said Badger, but I do think you should be more careful in future about going into holes Batman," "Oh I will, I promise," said Batman. "Thank you Badger for all your help," said Batman.

Excitement over for the day Violet and Batman left the Fire Hills for home and a welcome dinner.

VIOLET & YOGI

"Yogi Yogi where are you?"

Yogi came bounding down the stairs, tail swishing from side to side hearing his mummy's voice. "Yogi we are going to see your cousin Violet today. You know what a mischievous little Pug she is. I don't want her leading you astray. Is that clear?"

Yogi, a springer spaniel, was not averse to being mischievous himself and getting into scrapes. He loved water and at the first opportunity he would lunge himself into any pond or lake he saw and swim wildly.

Then, would shake himself to dry off normally by the nearest person in sight.

Violet's mummy never told Violet that anyone was coming to see her until the very last moment. She didn't want Violet plotting her next adventure too soon.

"Violet your cousin Yogi is coming to see you today," said her mummy, "Please don't get up to mischief with him," Pleaded her mummy. "He doesn't need to be led astray by you."

As soon as Violet heard the name Yogi her mind started to go into overdrive. "Right" she immediately thought, 'I think I know exactly what we shall do." Violet had to smother her elation at the thought of seeing Yogi again. Too much excitement and her mummy would guess immediately what she was up to. Nonchalantly Violet walked over to her bed trying hard to look disinterested, but all the time her mind was racing.

The excitement was gradually getting the better of her so she decided a walk in the garden was the best option right now. "What great news this is," thought Violet, "I had better finalise my plans for our adventure."

Yogi too was excited and paced up and down in the car until his mummy shouted at him to sit still. "We shall soon be there," She said.

No sooner had the car come to a halt in the drive Yogi leapt out and bounced up the garden looking for Violet. "Violet where are you, "he shouted.

Violet had been deep in thought and jumped when she heard Yogi's voice.

"Hello Yogi I'm over here," she replied by the big wooden swing seat.

"It's a long time since we've seen each other Yogi," said Violet. "Yes it is, but what are we going to do today Violet?" Replied Yogi in a somewhat impatient tone. "How would you like to go to the beach?" said Violet. "I was hoping you would suggest that," said Yogi starting to brim with excitement.

Hello, Violet whose your friend," squawked the Seagull sitting on the roof of the neighbouring bungalow. Both Violet and Yogi looked up at the imperious looking Seagull. "Hello Mr Seagull, this is my cousin Yogi we are just off to the beach" replied Violet. "Well, have fun" said Mr Seagull as he spread his wings and flew high into the bright blue sky.

"Now follow me Yogi, there's a hole under the fence at the back of the garden we will need to slide under." One by one they squeezed through the hole to the other side and the two cousins then trotted off down the lane towards the woods and eventually the sea!

They had no sooner reached the entrance to the woods when from out of nowhere a huge silver grey Husky skidded to a halt in front of them frightening both Violet and Yogi. "Oh, it's you Wally, you made us jump," said Violet. "Sorry" said Wally in a squeaky voice. "This is my cousin Yogi we are going to the beach," said Violet.

"Hello Wally," said Yogi, "that's a funny name for a dog of your size if you don't mind me saying, why did they name you Wally?" "I think it's because I am always doing silly things Yogi, I've also got this funny voice as well. Can I come to the beach with you? "Wally squeaked?" "Yes, of course you can, come on let's go," said Violet.

The three dogs made their way along the cliff path through the trees until they reached the beach. "Ah, that's good, the tide is still out but you must follow me as there are muddy spots that you sink in, "said Violet. Yogi by now was getting more and more excited at the sight of the water. Unable to contain himself any longer he flew past Violet, and with one huge leap landed with a mighty thud in the mud. Yogi could not free himself and was firmly stuck! "Why didn't you listen to me Yogi?

Now you can see what I was saying about the mud," Violet shouted at him this time.The sight of the three dogs with one stuck firmly in the mud soon began to draw attention. A man with a rope came over and said to Yogi, "grab this with your teeth and I will try and pull you out." Pull as he could, Yogi remained firmly entrenched.

"Don't go away I'll be right back," said the man. "That's a funny thing to say me being stuck solid in this mud," thought Yogi." Yogi was starting to panic now he didn't want to die as the sea would certainly take him if he didn't get rescued soon. But, true to his words the man returned bringing with him another man, who had a long pole.

The man with pole then looked around him until he found a huge rock that he manoeuvred into position on the sand close to Yogi. The man with the rope said " I want you to grab the rope with your teeth again and you two pull, looking at Violet and Wally while we push down on the pole. We are going to try and lever you out Yogi. There isn't much time before the tide starts coming in," said the man.

Yogi grabbed the rope as he was told and the two men started to push the pole into the mud under Yogi's tummy, "here goes, " said the man as he lowered the pole onto the rock and with Violet and Wally pulling gave one big push and an awful sucking noise Yogi rose from the mud and flew into the air landing on the soft sand.

"Oh thank you so much," said the grateful Yogi, "yes thank you for saving my cousin," yelled Violet. "Oh Yes, oh yes" squeaked Wally.

"You had better go and clean yourself up," said the man with pole. "Don't do it again," said the man with the rope. With that the two men disappeared.

"Yogi look at you, you are covered in mud let's get you into the sea to clean yourself up, come along and follow me," said Violet. This time Yogi obeyed Violet as she headed towards the now incoming tide.

"Don't be long Yogi, just clean yourself up and we will have to make our way home."

The three friends began making their way home through the woods until they reached the lane. "I'm off home now, bye," squeaked Wally and was gone.

The two tired cousins trundled back up the lane to the hole under the fence where they squeezed themselves back into the garden.

Arriving at the back door Violet shouted, "Is there any food? We're starving."

VIOLET, REGINALD & RUPERT

For Violet, every day was was an adventure, and today was not going to be any different. Today her two cousins Reginald and Rupert were going to be making a rare visit to see her. Reginald a huge 'Boxweiller' towered Violet, but was always kind and looked after her. Rupert the 'Boxer' was boisterous and liked to tease Violet, he was still very young but Reginald usually kept him in check.

"Violet come here I want to speak to you" said her mummy. "Here we go, another lecture," thought Violet. "Your two cousins are coming today and I want you to be on your best behaviour! You are not, and I repeat 'not,' to lead them astray, Violet." Violet turned her head away so that her mummy could not see the smirk on her face. "And don't stick your tongue out". A habit that Violet seemed to be doing a lot lately.

Violet had been planning an adventure with them as soon as her mummy told her they were coming. "Now go and play in the garden Violet until they arrive." With that Violet slowly walked out of the door and then raced as fast as she could to the bottom of the garden behind the barn where she could not be seen, to finalise her plans for the day.

"Violet, Violet where are you?" shouted Reginald and Rupert. Violet peered from behind the barn "I'm over here" replied Violet, "come and join me said Violet."

"What are you doing down here" said Rupert. "I am planning what we are going to do today, but I don't want my parents finding out, otherwise they will put a stop to it. So we must be very quiet!" Violet whispered. "What are we going to do then "said Rupert, whispering so softly Violet could barely make out what he was saying.

"You two like swimming in the sea don't you?" said Violet "Yes,Yes" shouted both Reginald and Rupert. "Shush," said Violet trying to contain their excitement.

"Well" said Violet, "there is a path very close that goes down the cliff to the beach. If we are careful it won't take us too long to get there. We must be very careful though."

"That sounds great Violet," said Reginald. "There is no wind today so the sea should be very calm," said Violet. "But the gate is bolted, how are we going to get out?" said Rupert.

"Ah! This is where we need Reginald's help! You are big Reginald. Do you think you can reach up and undo the bolt?" said Violet

"That shouldn't be a problem" said Reginald.

"We must be very careful and quiet going by the house so that we are not seen or heard," said Violet.

"If you two are ready, I'll go first just to see if the 'coast is clear' and will then beckon you down."

With that, Violet walked nonchalantly down the garden looking in the big patio doors where she couldn't see any activity. On reaching the side gate, she turned and beckoned the other two who quickly set about getting to the gate as quickly as possible.

Reginald looked at the bolt on the gate, stretched himself up to his great height, and slid the bolt along with ease. They were out, free!

"Follow me," said Violet as the three of them trotted down the road on the start of their adventure, an adventure that would live with them for the rest of their lives.

Violet led the way as the three of them with great excitement made their way along the lanes towards the wood that led them to the path and the steps that would take them to the beach. Both Reginald and Rupert were surprised by the many steps they had to negotiate, but the sight of the sea encouraged them on their downward journey.

"I don't know how you manage all these steps with your small legs Violet" said Rupert. "I've been down here a few times," said the now 'puffing' Violet. "I will be glad when we get to the bottom though," Violet retorted!

Step by step the three cousins descended down until they reached the pebbles of the beach. "Oh thank goodness we are here, even with my long legs that was exhausting," said Reginald "Look at that water it's so calm and looks inviting," cried Rupert "Let's all go in together," said a now very excited Reginald. "You two go in and enjoy ourselves; you know I don't like water," said Violet. "We will look after you Violet," said Rupert.

Violet was having nothing of their promises; she knew that once they were in the water they would swim off and leave her. "No I'm not going in," Violet's tone was now sterner now. "Ok we'll have a nice swim and cool off and promise we will be careful," said Reginald in a now conciliatory tone of voice.

Violet always had a strong dislike for water from a very young age. She would avoid puddles and even walk around them, rather than get her paws wet. A source of amusement to her friends.

Violet watched on as Reginald and Rupert splashed and swam in the calm blue waters.

"Don't go too far out," she shouted as the two heads of her cousins bounced about in the water.

Eventually the two brothers clambered out of the water and up the beach to where Violet was seated. "Oh that was brilliant," said Reginald. "We both enjoyed that so much Violet, thank you for suggesting this adventure, "said Rupert. "Well, once you have dried off we will have to make our way home," said Violet.

The two brothers stretched their wet bodies on the beach soaking up the summer sun whilst they dried off. Reginald was the first to get up stretching his long legs, "come on Rupert wakey wakey," he said. Rupert with a big yawn dragged his now dry body from the pebbles, "yes I suppose we should make a move, I'm not looking forward to all those steps are you Reginald," he said. "Not really Rupert, I don't know how poor old Violet copes with her short legs," Reginald replied.

Violet overhearing this conversation butted in, "I've done this lots of times and quite used to it now," she said.

"Right, let's go otherwise we are all going to get into trouble!" said Violet. The three cousins trundled over the pebbles to where the steps started for their ascent up the cliff.

They were about halfway up the steps with Violet leading and Rupert at the rear and somewhat lagging well behind.

"Come on Rupert catch up," shouted Violet. It was at this point Violet became conscious of some funny noises all around her. The noises became louder and louder and the ground around the steps started to shake with such ferocity, Violet screamed, "what's happening I'm so frightened."

Reginald ran to Violet pushing her with such strength that they both rolled into the bracken just as the steps fell away.

"Rupert, Rupert where's Rupert," they both shouted at once. Peering over a now very steep cliff edge where the steps used to be they could just make out a large rock sticking out and hanging precariously about to fall further down the cliff face and to their amazement Rupert managed to get a footing and was now firmly seated and marooned on the rock.

"Rupert don't move and we will get help," called Reginald.

The noise and the news that there had been a cliff fall brought people running out of their houses and peering over the place where some of the steps used to be.

"Help," cried Violet. "Help'" shouted Reginald "My brother Rupert is marooned onto a rock which is likely to fall." A voice from the top called "can you two get to the top?" "Yes we will be alright and coming up now, "said Violet.

With careful manoeuver Violet and Reginald slowly but surely edged their way up the cliff side and were welcomed to the top by the now large crowd.

At that point, Violet and Reginald heard the noise of the oncoming coastguard helicopter. The thud thud of the massive rotors overhead caused a downdraught with dust swirling all-around. The crowds that had gathered started to disperse to get away from the ever-increasing storm of dust and flying objects. Violet could just make out the figure of someone hanging on the outside of the helicopter hooked up and about to be lowered down the rock face.

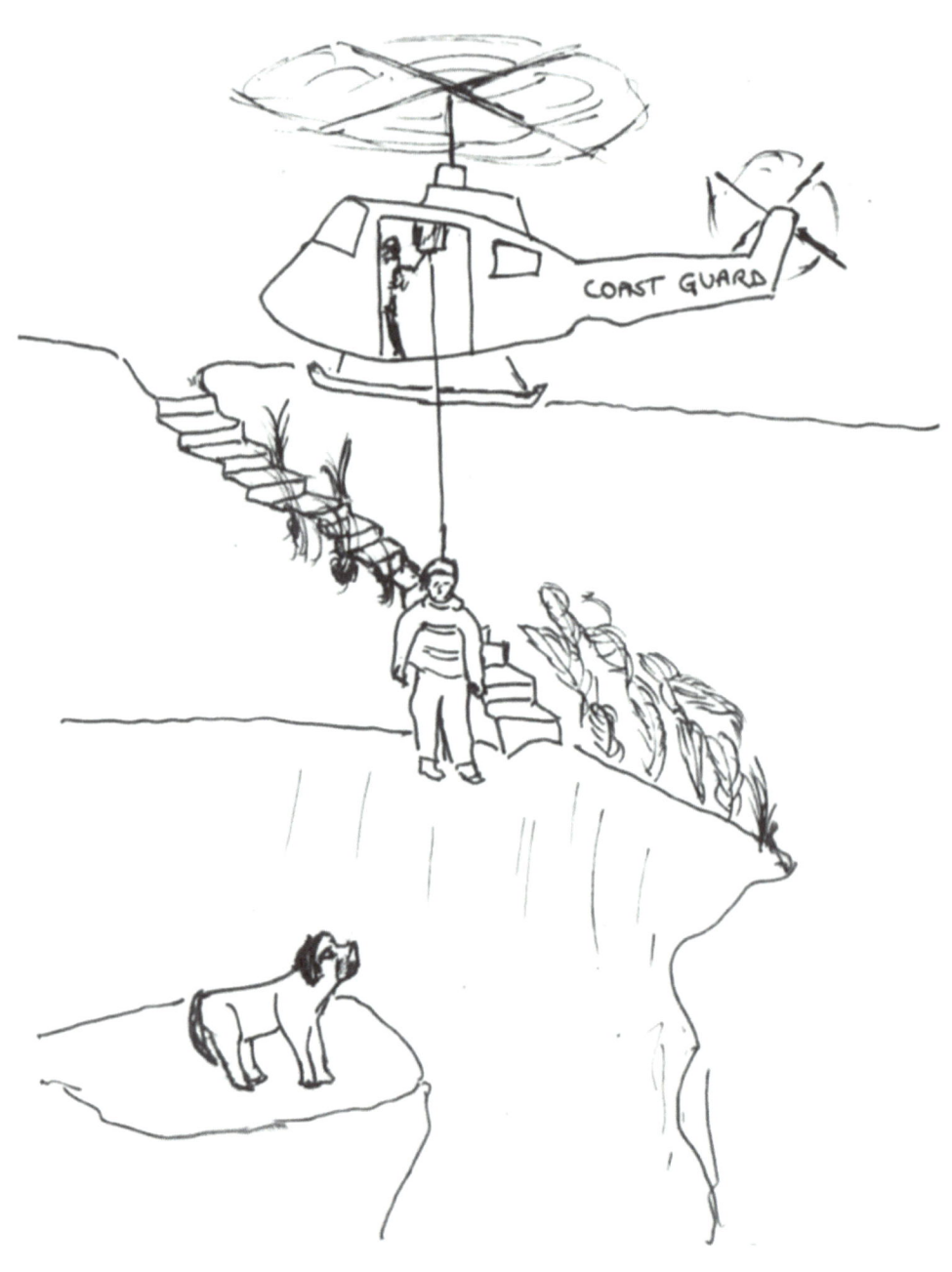

A rather tall policeman looked down on both Violet and Reginald and said "you two had better scarper off home, the coastguard is going to try and rescue your friend and we will bring him home to you. I assume you live locally?" "Yes that's right officer here's my address," said Violet as the policeman wrote it down.

Without further delay, Violet and Reginald left for home at full speed. They just arrived at the gate when again they heard the sound of the helicopter overhead just to see the man again being lowered onto the drive this time with Rupert in his arms.

"How are we going to explain this," said a rather rueful Reginald with a very hangdog face!

VIOLET & THE SNOWMAN

The December skies were dark and the thickening clouds were soon to unleash the first of the winter snows.

The temperature was falling fast as the afternoon daylight faded slowly into early evening. In the distance the faint rumbling of the big trucks could be heard discharging their cargoes of salt on the roads in the hope of melting the impending snow before it turned into ice.

"Have you got the snow shovels ready at hand?" Violets mummy said to her husband? "Everything is ready, stop fussing. If we are lucky we might get away with just a light dusting," said her husband.

"Snow dusting," thought Violet, "What strange words! I haven't heard those before! I don't know why they seem to be so busy this evening, perhaps they must be expecting something!" With that Violet laid her head down again in the warmth of her bed.

By 10 'O'clock in the evening the first flurries of snow started to descend. The sky and surrounding landscapes seemed to light up as the tiny drops of white crystals cascaded down before becoming larger and thicker until they resembled big cotton wool balls. She heard her mummy calling from the back door to her daddy, "It's getting very thick out here!"

Violet's curiosity eventually got the better of her as she stood by the big glass door watching everything around being covered by this white stuff! "I wonder what it is," she mused! "I must say it does look inviting to play in!"

"Violet, quickly you must go in the garden before the snow gets too deep before bedtime!" Violet took one look at this 'white stuff' and turned to go back in doors.

"No, out you go now," said her mummy giving Violet a push at the same time. Violet sank into this white stuff up to the tops of her paws and decided she wouldn't spend long outside. Violet was pleased to get back indoors in the warmth and to her bed. "Did you like the snow Violet?" her mummy said. "Oh, so that's what it's called," said Violet turning to look up at her mummy. "It's very soft and very cold," replied Violet as she made her way back to her bed for the night.

The snow fell heavily through the night piling up against the doors. It was as much as Violet's daddy could do to get outside and clear a way through, but paths were cleared and high piles of snow now covered the garden flower beds.

"Do you want to go in the garden Violet," said her mummy I will have to put your coat on first. With that Violet gently took her second outing into the snow.

"Ooh this is cold on my paws," she thought.

"I don't think I will stay out here too long" as she gently walked into the garden.

Violet suddenly jumped high into the air, not through excitement or happiness, but fear! Something large was on the lawn, all white with a funny hat on and a nose that resembled a carrot! "What can it be," she thought now shivering quite uncontrollably. Violet couldn't take her eyes off this object and stood from afar not daring to go any closer. Slowly, as her confidence returned her curiosity started to get the better of her, she moved closer towards this white object.

"Hello, Mr. White thing I haven't seen you before" said Violet! To Violet's amazement the white thing looked down at her with his funny looking eyes, "hello" he said "I'm a Snowman not a white thing, I am only allowed out when it's snowing, when the snow goes I go," he said. "Are You very cold Mr Snowman," said a now more confident Violet. "can I get you a nice hot drink?" Enquired Violet. "Don't be silly little dog, if I have a hot drink I will melt," came his rather gruff reply.

"Oh I am sorry I didn't think," timidly Violet replied. "you can get me a carrot if you don't mind the seagulls around here keep pecking at my nose and it won't be very long before it goes completely", said the snowman. "Yes of course, I'll bring you a spare one as well," said Violet as she ran in doors to find the carrots. "What are you rummaging for now Violet?" her mummy said.

"I need a carrot for the snowman's nose," Violet replied. "A snowman, is there a snowman in the garden then?" Violet's Mummy asked. "Yes he was there when I went out and asked for a new carrot nose, "said Violet. "There are plenty of carrots in the cupboard help yourself," Violet's mummy said.

Violet took two large carrots and returned to the garden and the snowman. "Here you are Mr. Snowman, two large carrots for you." "Oh thank you little dog you are so kind. What's your name," said the snowman?" "My name is Violet," She replied. "Well, thank you very much Violet," the snowman said now emphasising Violet's name. "Well, I shall come and see you every day that you are here," said Violet." I'm hoping for some cold weather for some time as it's nice being alive again," said Snowman.

Violet, kept her promise and paid the Snowman a visit each day, replacing his nose regularly as it kept disappearing daily now, not only were the seagulls feasting on his nose, but the pigeons also had joined in. Whenever Violet saw them feeding on her newfound friend she would chase them off by barking loudly at them.

"You are so kind to me Violet, I will miss you when I go," said the snowman. As each day passed, the weather continued to remain extremely cold and Violet and the Snowman's friendship grew and grew. "I don't know what I will do when the weather gets warmer and you have to go. I will miss you so much Mr. Snowman," said Violet.

Little did Violet realise that the weather was becoming milder and was due to become a lot warmer in the next few days. It was not until the following morning when Violet made her visit to Mr. Snowman and the sight of him melting away,

his eyes, now just watery dots, his nose or what was left just a few shreds of carrots, looked at Violet to make his last farewell. Violet couldn't believe what was happening, her big marble eyes now filled with tears crying, pleading with him not to go.

"Please, Please don't go," she cried and sobbed putting her paws around what was fast becoming a melting pool of ice. "Promise me you will come back again," she pleaded. The snowman looked at Violet for the last time and whispered, "I promise," before disappearing into a large puddle.

Violet's tears fell into the water that was once the spot where the snowman stood. Picking up his hat and the remains of what was once his nose, Violet whispered

"Goodbye my friend." as she tearfully went indoors.

Lightning Source UK Ltd.
Milton Keynes UK
UKHW050936200721
387439UK00002B/170